Love Between the Borderline

Jenna Cervantes

BookLeaf Publishing

India | USA | UK

Presentation by *BookLeaf Publishing*

Web: www.bookleafpub.com

E-mail: info@bookleafpub.com

ISBN: 9789363315983

First edition 2024

To my children, Christian, Janelle, and Hannah—you are my heart and my inspiration. Your unwavering love has been my guiding light. You made my life worth living.

To my mother, Karen Cervantes, and my sisters, Kimberly Tellez and Sarah Cervantes, thank you for your unconditional love and support throughout my ups and downs.

And to anyone on their own journey of recovery:

"Do not let anyone seal your fate, our own life is what we create."

ACKNOWLEDGEMENT

I would like to acknowledge my beautiful Nelly who stayed by my side throughout this process and painstakingly helped me edit and title my poems.

Juan Gonzalez, you believed in me and took the publisher bio picture before this book was even a reality. That gesture meant the world to me.

Richard Carl Cook[3], you have been my best cheerleader these past few years, always hyping me up and reminding me of my potential.
Thank You!!

And to all the people I've loved along the way, thank you for being part of my journey.

PREFACE

I have been in recovery for 18 years from Borderline Personality Disorder, a journey that has profoundly shaped my life. The doctor told me I would never recover, but I am proving him wrong every day. This book is the realization of a dream I had as a 10-year-old girl, a dream that has stayed with me and grown stronger over time.

This collection of love poetry is a testament to that dream. The poems within these pages are chosen for their ability to convey the tender and beautiful aspects of love. The darker, more intense poems I have written are saved for another day, reflecting a different part of my journey.

This book is my offering to the world, a piece of my heart and soul, shared with the hope that it brings warmth and understanding to those who read it.

WE DO RECOVER!!!

Decorum

I would mind my P's and Q's;
I am writing poetry again.
To go down infamously in cursive or print,
all of our moments down they went.
Impressed upon pages of turmoil and pain,
moments of clarity between the insane.
Nothing goes unnoticed.
I will bare it all.
After the flame the ashes fall
and all our love, left to recall.

Double Clove Hitch

Maybe I am chasing the wind,
nothing appears as it seems.
I feel as a rope
with frayed ends.

What kind of knots do you know
to tye me closely to your soul.
Will I unravel,
abandoned afloat?

If I move ever so slow as I go,
would you even notice?
Would you even know?

Leap of Faith

Engulfed in black and white thinking
my heart leapt up
high off the ledge
and pushed outward
beyond the confines of the ground
into the open air.
My motives as stifled as they may be
shine through translucently.
All that I feel
all that I love
all that is bound by me
falls to the ground.....

Safely.

Unfathomable

4

This morning felt like an infinite ocean of
bottomless tomorrows.
One by one leading themselves back to the sea
just as the tides do endlessly.

Obscure Internal Monolog

The voices in my head won't stop.
They bicker amongst eachother.
Mudsling and gouge eyes.
They are the angry words that break free of my
mind.

Escaping eagerly from my lips
to pierce straight through your heart with a
soiled blade.
Ultimately to infect your disposition and drive
you insane.

Hours will turn to days.
Days to weeks.
Weeks to months.
Months to years.
You will always remember the moment I sliced
through you.
My tongue sharp as a sword.
Without intent I butchered you,
and left you to be torn apart by scavengers along
the way side.

Allocation

I will not set fire to the words I have to say to
you.
I will extinguish the flames with affection.

This love will be set aside just for you,
as your portion.
No one will touch it!
Not even I.

Deep longing sigh......

To Be Kept

I love seeing a man clear out his brand new
fence line.

All those years of rambling,

finally the yearning
of wanting to be kept inside.

I Still Love You This Way

When the love of my life calls
I answer.
I hang on to every word,
so I can replay it over and over in my mind.
His voice soothes every ach I've ever known.
I wonder.... What would it be like
if he were mine?
To love.
To hold.
To kiss.
To hug.
I do not realize how much I miss him,
until he calls;
and I answer.
I will always answer.

Empath

You must be strong to love me I am not for the
weak.
Sometimes you must listen more than you speak.

Equipped with a tourniquet just in case,
I'm bleeding out all over the place,

from all of the trauma that I carry.
The ones that show and the ones that I bury.

You must be gentle in words and deeds.
These things will cover most of my needs.

Hold me tight when I need your embrace.
Allow me to adoringly gaze upon your face.

Let me to be who I am to be,
wild at heart and unapologetically free.

Do not bind me up so no one can see
all the love and tenderness that's held within me.

For I am a healer of broken souls.
How this came to be no one knows.

Except for me and the little girl I was,
told to do what was said and not as one does.

She ran away to another land.
Deep inside her mind where there was no hand.
To hold or wipe away her tears.
To consoleingly explain her innermost fears.

She grew up quick and she grew up tall,
holding it together consoling them all.

Yellow

It remained heavy on my soul
when you said you are not happy.
I thought about your smile
and how I wished for it to stay.
On your lips.
In your eyes.
For that feeling to never go away.

I wondered what it is inside your mind
that made your edges fray?
What is it you long for when you're alone?
What are the things that make your world grey?

I thought about your favorite color,
yellow is what you said.
What is it that turns grey to yellow inside your
head?
What are the simple things that force you out of
bed?
To face the day with pleasure and not with dred.

Happiness can be found in minescule things.
Like watching the ocean
and finding the treasure it brings.

Happiness in the night sky;
gazing at the stars.
You sit looking up into the past,
while present time in ours.

Happiness in nature while sitting in a field,
listening to birds gather up their yield.

The rain that patters down on your roof,
while tucked in cozy these things are proof.

Happiness comes in all sorts of ways.
It may not be ever present,
it doesn't always stay.

But finding it again is not too hard,
when you love insignificant things
in the best regard.

Let it not be fleeting,
alluring you into the dark.

When something new can catch your eye,
as simple as it seems;
take a moment to find happiness even in the
minutest of things.

Divine Feminine

I am loved beyond measure,
people are drawn to me.
People are touched by my deep feminine energy.

It is a magnet that pulls
manifesting things to me.

I bring light to darkness,
giving love to the heartless.
The kind of love that drowns self doubt
and emerges seeds of tenderness to sprout.

I will always be felt with out touch.
Seen without being visible.
Heard with the echos of my existing force.
I will remain in the stillframes
of your mind.
Until your last breath serves your lungs with life.

I am a divine feminine woman,
I embody all that I am to become.

June 16, 2024

I's ok
to ache a little,
to feel somber.
To feel the empty space,
a space as big as the sky.
Turquoise and blue,
sometimes pink and orange.

But today it's dark
like it's going to pour
deep down in my heart.
The place where I kept you near
when you were gone.

Your smile is clear in my mind.
Teeth like pearls.
Your hands always rough
as they held mine, so tiny.

The things I love and hate about you
reside in me.
Because I am your daughter.... you see.

I remember the dreams you instilled into my
soul.

You taught me how to fly.
Now that you're gone I soar.

I thank you for all of those things
you didn't know you were teaching,
like how to mourn those we lose,
and how to pray.

Beneath it all
I am Your daughter.
Your blood runs through my veins
and keeps me alive every day.

I will live without you and wonder;
do you miss me?
Do you feel a missing piece?

Or am I the only one living this way?
For I know there are two other souls
that share the same dismay.
Your daughters.....

Self-Soothe

I feel so alone.
The urgency to weep creeps up my esophagus
and my throat gets tight.

I feel the tears start to form in my eyelids
I am undoubtedly beside myself.

I comfort a little girl who knows not how strong
she will be,
one day when there is no choice but to be strong.

I am breaking a little piece at a time
soon I will be dust that lingers on the ground.

I will gather myself back to the earth
and become whole again.

The Girl Who Loved A Dragon

I wondered why it was so hard to love him.
I poured out my healing waters repeatedly
over his self rightousness and loathing.

I extinguished the flames of the vices he sought.
I encouraged the deep meaningful desires he
reflected onto me.

I sought out his darkness,
while I carried a lamp to light each crevise
inside his mind.

I lowered my eyes so I would not intimidate
him.
He was so easily spooked with intimacy or
anything that reminded him to feel.

A bottomless pit of anguish is what he carried.
 A void of strangled dreams and rotting
aspirations dangled from his feet.....

He kept himself high.
So high... I could not see his face,
or recognize the silloute that lingered.

That silloute over shadowed me intensely.
It kept me in the dark with only my lantern to
keep me warm and alert.
I was hypervigilant to the storms inside his
heart.

He breathed out through his jowles heavy like a
dragon,
emotionless and fearlessly ready to consume me.

The flames blazed,
charring my skin.
I would raise my arms to protect myself from
being insinerated,
even annihilated completely.

In the end,
before I realized it was the end;
I rose up like a pheonix and I shined the light
inside my soul so blindingly
it caught the dragon offguard.

I escaped with my life.
Myself along with three souls went running off
into the night,
sobbing while fleeing the cage we were kept.

We survived.
In the end we survived!!!!

Enmity

The angst creeps up into my throat.
Here it goes,
I'm about to fucking blow.
Eyes dilate,
spit coming forth from my mouth.
Rage burns red,
no more black and white.
Just pure disgusting hatred that robs me of my
peace.
Crimson furiosity fills the marrow of my bones
and spills into my blood.
It boils into a violent pool where I will drown
you.
I will drown me.
And we will be scorched into a volatile vapor of
despairing nothing.

Insignia

I hate having people in my life that I can not
trust,
because I hand out trust in beautiful envelopes.
Envelopes with a golden seal stamped upon the
back.
It displays my initials,
J.L.C. in cursive;
the way a queens seal should be.
Some carefully open it so not to damage the seal
and others ravage it to shreds.
They gaze up at me very curiously,
seeking to know the information beseeched
inside.
I look down in pity at the fool in front of me
and in that moment I realize......
I cast my pearls before swine.

Evanesce

I am lost again.
In the depths of my heart
and the corridors of my mind.

I call out,
I hear only echos.

You,
 I can not find.

With one hand I reach to where you were,
my other finger tip still dragging along the wall.

 I can not see,
 it is dark.

I am disoriented
in this still and the very quiet empty void you
disappeared into.

You...
left me here,
intently scowering for those beautiful eyes of
blue.

Let Love Be Enough

Let me love you
the way I know how.
My love heals all it touches,
calms aches that have lingered
and quenches thirsts that saturate deep down into
the marrow.
Let me hold you....
You will feel the insurmountable love that exists
in my being
and be bathed in the most valuable thing I have
to offer,
LOVE.....

R.C.C.[3]

There is no need to fear
what could there be?
When I have a friend like you
who took interest in me.

A light in the darkness
when my eyes are closed tight.
A voice in the emptiness of a lonely night.

Someone I can reach out to
and will never refrain,
always with comfort consoling my pain.

Someone I can turn to
no need to explain.
Ready and able
without restrain.

Thank you tremendously
for being there for me.
In times of doubt.
In times of need.

I smile knowing there's someone like you.
Through the black and white
you have helped me through.

Ode on Sleepless Nights

25

Every evening when you were away,
I would lay in bed at night and say.....
Good night my love,
in your dreams,
as you sleep.
May my kisses fall
on your lips silently.

I Love You

I love you
How do I know?

Because of the safety I feel in our space
and the comfort I feel in your embrace.

The electricity that pulses through the marrow of
my bones,
I recall it often when I am alone.

The deep sigh that emmerges when you reach
for my hand.
The way you always seem to understand.

To sit in silence is important to me.
We do this togther effortlessly.

The way my heart leaps after we kiss;
Proof to me my love exists.

Its more than your sexuality that arouses me.
It's the peace in your presence that surrounds
me.

And I feel loved there.

www.ingramcontent.com/pod-product-compliance
Lightning Source LLC
LaVergne TN
LVHW021331200726
843509LV00014B/2494